Salmon Stream

By Carol Reed-Jones
Illustrations by Michael S. Maydak

Dawn Publications

This is the stream in the forest.

This is the water, clear and cool,
that flows in the stream in the forest.

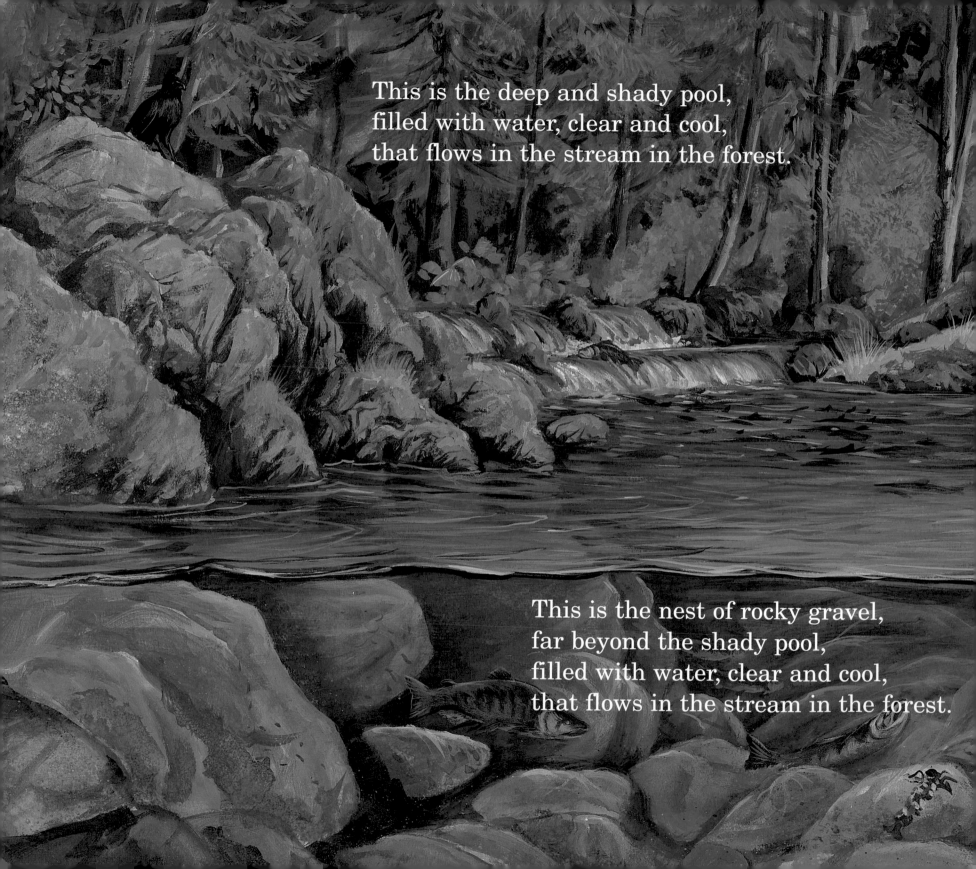

This is the deep and shady pool,
filled with water, clear and cool,
that flows in the stream in the forest.

This is the nest of rocky gravel,
far beyond the shady pool,
filled with water, clear and cool,
that flows in the stream in the forest.

The egg of a salmon, born to travel,
hides in the nest of rocky gravel,
far beyond the shady pool,
filled with water, clear and cool,
that flows in the stream in the forest.

This is the tiny fish that hatched
(and has its dinner still attached),
from the egg of a salmon, born to travel,
that hides in the nest of rocky gravel
far beyond the shady pool,
filled with water, clear and cool,
that flows in the stream in the forest.

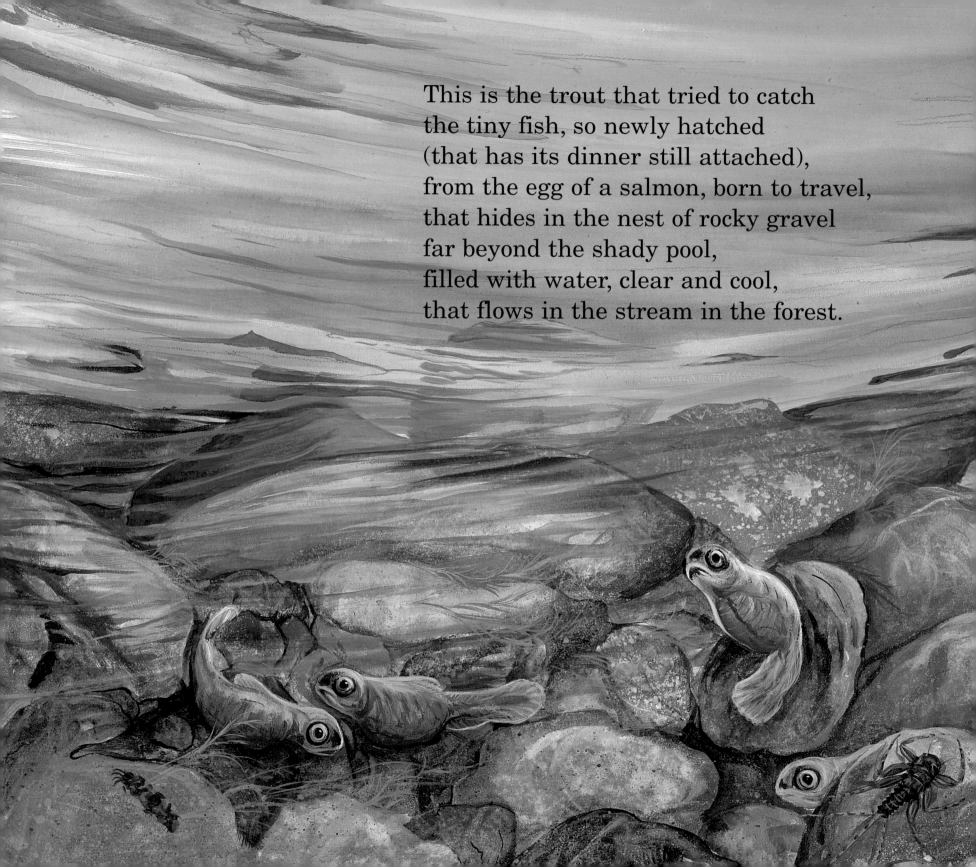

This is the trout that tried to catch
the tiny fish, so newly hatched
(that has its dinner still attached),
from the egg of a salmon, born to travel,
that hides in the nest of rocky gravel
far beyond the shady pool,
filled with water, clear and cool,
that flows in the stream in the forest.

A hovering osprey dived to snatch
the wily trout that tried to catch
the tiny fish, so newly hatched
(that has its dinner still attached),
from the egg of a salmon, born to travel,
that hides in the nest of rocky gravel
far beyond the shady pool,
filled with water, clear and cool,
that flows in the stream in the forest.

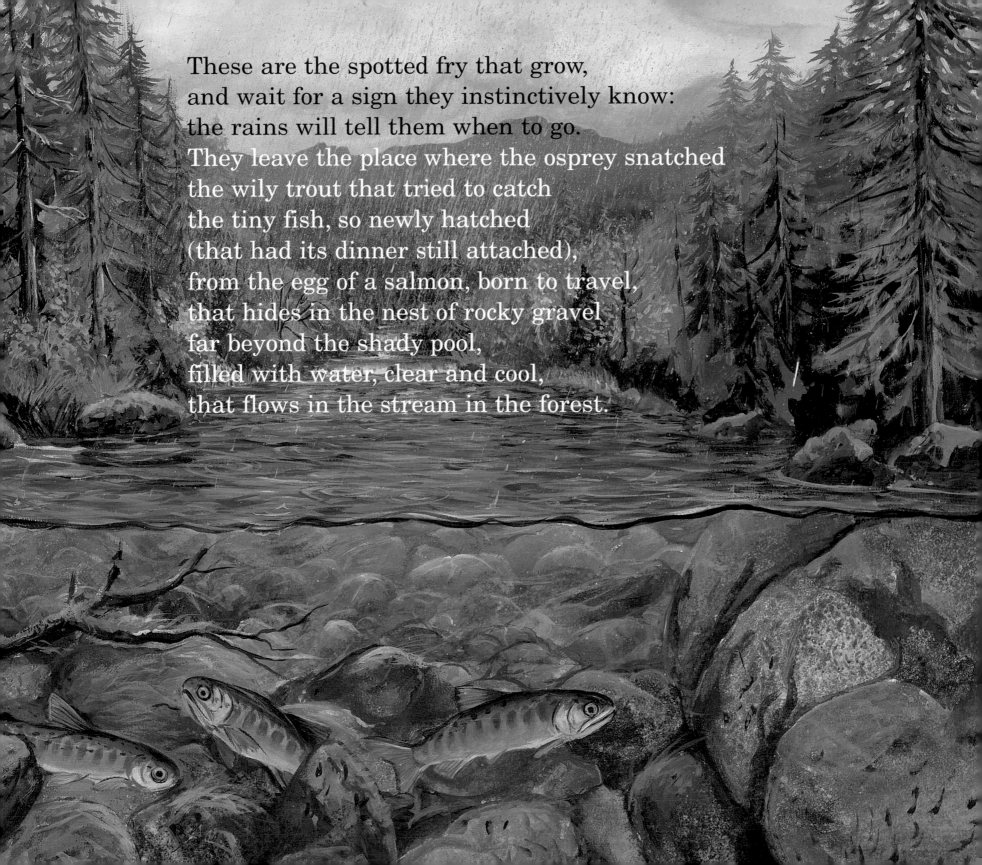

These are the spotted fry that grow,
and wait for a sign they instinctively know:
the rains will tell them when to go.
They leave the place where the osprey snatched
the wily trout that tried to catch
the tiny fish, so newly hatched
(that had its dinner still attached),
from the egg of a salmon, born to travel,
that hides in the nest of rocky gravel
far beyond the shady pool,
filled with water, clear and cool,
that flows in the stream in the forest.

Traveling down with the current's flow,
facing upstream as they go,
the smolt pass obstacles great and small,
gravelly shallows, a waterfall,
through culverts and pipes devised by man,
down a fish ladder on a dam,
and to an estuary wide.

Drifting with the ebbing tide,
they reach their saltwater home at last,
an ocean indescribably vast.

The salmon grow for months in the sea,
catching fish and swimming free,

Coho Salmon

Steelhead Trout

Chinook Salmon

Pink Salmon

Sockeye

Chum

Atlantic Salmon

trying not to become a meal
for human, sea lion, orca or seal,
until they get the homing urge
to gather where river and ocean merge.

This is the rain that swells the rivers,
and sends the message that nature delivers
to salmon to send them home to spawn,
relentlessly swimming on and on—
up the river with the tide,
past the estuary wide . . .

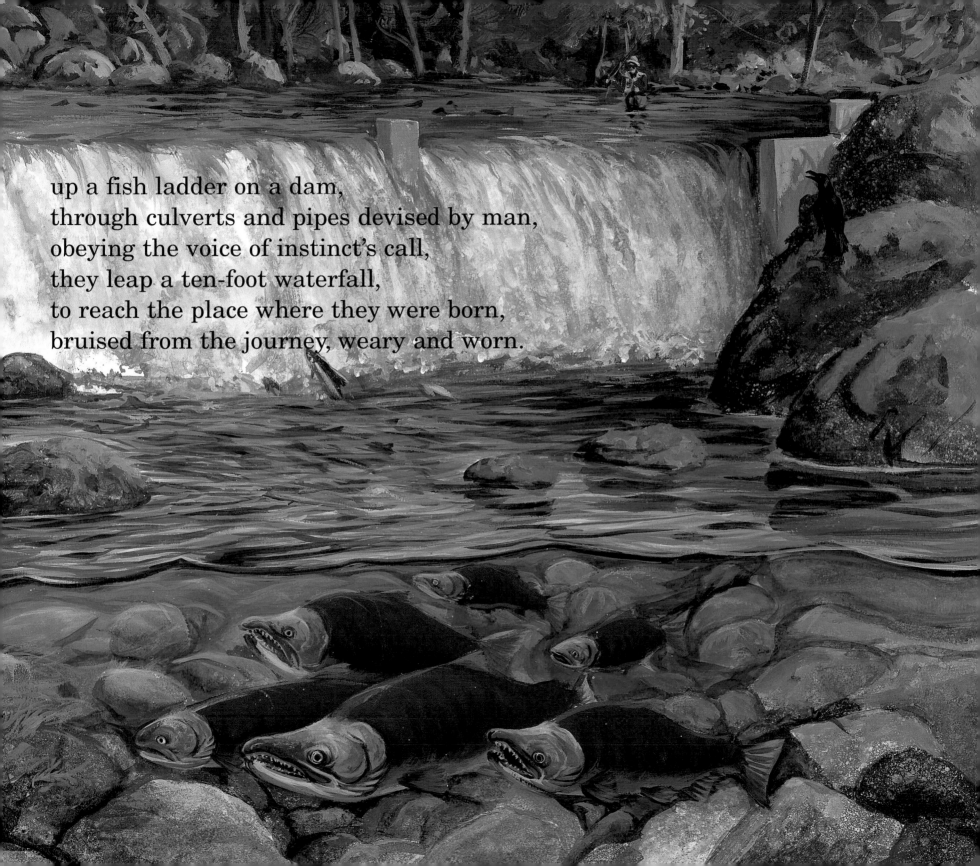

up a fish ladder on a dam,
through culverts and pipes devised by man,
obeying the voice of instinct's call,
they leap a ten-foot waterfall,
to reach the place where they were born,
bruised from the journey, weary and worn.

The salmon come home at the end of their lives.
They spawn, and each little egg that survives
will start the cycle over again
with the coming of the rain,
and silver smolt will discover the sea
and turn to salmon swimming free,
and tiny fish will one day hatch
(with their dinners still attached)
from the eggs of a salmon, born to travel,
that hide in the nest of rocky gravel
far beyond the shady pool,
filled with water, clear and cool,
that flows in the stream in the forest.

The Salmon Cycle

Life for wild salmon begins and ends in a stream. Salmon hatch in fresh water, but migrate to the ocean, where they mature in salt water. Then the salmon return to spawn, usually in the very same stream where they hatched. Fish that do this are called *anadromous*.

In the gravel of a streambed, the female salmon begins to dig a nest with strong flips of her tail. While she is digging the nest, spawning males compete with each other to be the one to fertilize the eggs she will lay. Every spawning female salmon has thousands of eggs in her body. When the nest is dug, the female lays hundreds of pinkish-orange round eggs, each about the size of a pea. The male salmon fertilizes the eggs by squirting them with milt, a milky substance.

The eggs are soft when they are first laid, almost like blobs of jelly, and will stick to any surface they touch shortly after they are laid. They settle into spaces between the rocks, where flowing water brings vital oxygen to the eggs. The female covers the eggs with gravel, then moves a little farther upstream to dig another nest and repeat the process all over again. Except for sockeye, each mating pair of salmon makes a group of several nests, called a *redd*. A sockeye redd has just one nest.

Within about an hour, each egg absorbs water and becomes firm, or *water-hardened*, protecting the developing salmon inside. Still, there are many predators; only about two out of every 3,000 eggs laid survive to become a spawning adult salmon. The eggs stay hidden in the gravel from one to four months, until they hatch. Now they are called *alevins* (AL-uh-vins).

Each alevin has a yolk sac attached to its belly. Alevins do not have to hunt for food until they have used up all the yolk sac. After that, they are called *fry*, or *parr*. The fry emerge from the gravel to catch aquatic insects and insect larvae for food. Some fry develop spots and vertical stripes called *parr marks* that help camouflage them from predators. Pinks and Chums do not; they are spotless and silvery, and migrate to the ocean soon after they emerge from the streambed gravel. Other fry such as Coho or Chinook may remain in the stream for a year or more before migrating. Some Atlantic salmon stay in the parr stage from two to six years.

By the time the fry are ready to begin migrating to the ocean, their bodies have developed so that they will be able to make the change from fresh to salt water. They are called *smolts* at this stage. Rain is often the signal for smolts to begin migrating downstream to the ocean, traveling by night, hiding and resting in pools by day. If they are forced to linger too long in any resting place along the way to the ocean, they may lose the urge to migrate. Dams can cause this kind of delay; then the smolts may not complete the cycle and spawn.

To get to the ocean, the smolts swim through an *estuary*, a coastal wetland where fresh and salt water mingle. The smolts may stay in the estuary for a while to get used to salt water before swimming out into the ocean.

Once in the ocean, the juvenile salmon migrate far from the estuary as they grow to be adults. This can take several years, depending upon the type of salmon they are. Salmon migrate hundreds, sometimes even thousands of miles, in their lives. Young salmon eat plankton, tiny fish, and invertebrates such as shrimp. As they grow larger, some salmon species eat anchovies and herring. They will need to be large and strong for the long journey home.

Adult salmon, ranging from 18 to 48 inches long, instinctively know when it is time to migrate back to their home streams. Their extraordinary sense of smell guides them to the mouth of the river or stream where they first entered the ocean. They gather there, waiting. The first rain of the season is often the signal for them to start the journey home, called a salmon run. Once they start swimming upstream to spawn, salmon do not eat. They lose up to one-third of their body weight during the journey. The salmon's skin grows thicker and their scales disappear. The males develop hooked jaws, the sure sign of a spawner.

During their run, salmon swim upstream, resting in pools when they need to regain their strength. The salmon now jump over obstacles that were easier to pass going downstream. Chinooks and Atlantics have been seen leaping as high as ten to eleven feet to get over waterfalls and other things in their way. (Not all salmon are great leapers; Chums have trouble jumping more than three feet.) The urge to return is so strong that salmon risk everything to go home. Some die just trying.

After spawning, Pacific salmon (except Steelhead) will die within a week or two. Only Atlantics and Steelhead can migrate back to the ocean and later return to their home stream to spawn again.

About one Atlantic salmon in ten will survive another migration cycle to return and spawn a second time, and a few can return up to four additional times. Steelhead can return up to two or three times.

Throughout their lives, and after they die, salmon are part of the food chain for 137 known species. Even when they are dead, the salmon play a very important role in the ecosystem. Salmon carcasses return vital nutrients to the stream. Bears, ravens, crows, coyotes, raccoons, river otters, mink, eagles, gulls, and even insects eat the carcasses. Some insects feeding on the carcasses produce larvae that salmon fry will eat when they emerge from their gravel nests. If a salmon is able to return to its spawning grounds, the cycle can begin all over again.

Native peoples recognized the significance of the salmon's life cycle centuries ago, and treated it with reverence, taking only those fish that they needed. Everything salmon need, we also need: clean water, oxygen, forests, and safe places to live. We need salmon, and salmon need us to take care of the oceans, rivers and streams. That way they can continue their amazing life cycle.◆

Types of Salmon

Type	Life span	Average # eggs laid
Pink or Humpy	2 years	1,200-1,900
Silver or Coho	3 years	1,900-5,000
Chum or Dog	3 to 5 years	2,100-3,600
Sockeye or Red	4 years	2,800-4,000
Steelhead	3 to 6 years	3,000-3,500*
Chinook or King	3 to 7 years	3,000-7,000
Atlantic	6 to 15 years	4,000-16,000**

*Steelhead were once considered a trout, but scientists now classify them with Pacific salmon.
**Atlantic Salmon can live longer than Pacific salmon, 6 to 10 years on average. A salmon that survives to spawn a second time has had time in the ocean to grow larger than it was the first time it spawned, and can lay more eggs. Females can have up to 800 eggs per pound of body weight, so one 20-pound fish can lay as many as 16,000 eggs!

Did You Know?

Some salmon live in lakes and do not go to the ocean. Their bodies do not have to make the changes to salt water that ocean-migrating salmon must make.

What Makes a Good Salmon Stream?

▲ OXYGEN, COLD WATER AND SHADE. Salmon need plenty of oxygen to live, and they get all their oxygen from the water. When a salmon opens its mouth, water flows through its gills, which take oxygen out of the water the way that the lungs of land animals take oxygen from the air. Salmon must have cold water; it has more oxygen than warm water. Salmon are most at home in water that is cooler than 60° Fahrenheit (about 16° Celsius). Warmer water speeds up a fish's metabolism, making it breathe faster and use up more oxygen. But warmer water has less oxygen in it, so a salmon in warm water is a double loser. Shade helps by cooling the water and keeping its oxygen content high. Forests provide shade for streams and rivers. Also, oxygen is added to water when it flows over fallen trees, rocks, waterfalls and riffles. *Riffles* are rocky shallows where the water flows swiftly, making little waves and putting more oxygen into the water.

▲ CLEAN GRAVEL. Salmon need to lay their eggs in clean gravel without silt. Silt is soil dissolved in water. Silt can smother salmon eggs or alevin. It clogs the gills of older fish, too, so that they can't breathe—very bad for fish! Forests help to prevent silt as the roots of trees and other vegetation keep the soil in place.

▲ FREE-FLOWING RIVERS. Salmon need a clear path to and from the ocean. When a dam is built without a *fish ladder*—a series of shallow pools to help fish continue upstream—that salmon run becomes extinct. Migrating salmon are on a tight schedule, whether they are smolts or spawners. Even with fish ladders, dams may slow spawners down so much in their journey homeward that they die before they reach the spawning grounds. If there isn't enough water flowing down the fish ladder, the salmon may not use it, or even find it. If the fish ladder is too steep, or doesn't have enough resting places, the salmon may tire and take too long, or they may not get all the way up the ladder before dying. Salmon may also become confused by dams with large reservoirs, and be unable to find the current so that they can continue their journey.

▲ POOLS. Salmon need pools and ponds where they can rest and hide from predators. Trees that fall in streams form pools. Beavers build dams that create ponds. Where there is a waterfall or other obstacle, the salmon need a deep pool just below to help them leap up and over. Fish biologists have found that salmon need water that is one and a quarter times as deep as the height they have to jump. For example, if a salmon is going to jump over a ten-foot barrier, it needs to jump from a pool that is at least twelve and a half feet deep.

▲ FOOD. Young salmon eat aquatic insects and larvae. These insects and larvae, in turn, depend on nutrients that seep into the water from organic matter such as leaves, fallen submerged trees and the decaying carcasses of spawned-out salmon.

▲ CLEAN WATER. Salmon can't live in polluted water. That is where humans can help a lot. One elementary school adopted a stream, cleaned it up, tested the water for pollution, and raised salmon in their classroom to release into the stream. Two and a half years later, salmon returned to spawn there—in a stream that had not had any salmon for over twenty years! The story is told in the book, *Come Back, Salmon,* by Molly Cone. When we take care of the Earth's precious water supply, we benefit as much as the salmon do. ◆

How You Can Help

There are many organizations that work to help salmon. Native tribal fisheries do a lot of work to improve stream habitat and restore salmon runs. No matter what your age is, or where you live, there are ways that you can help salmon. Here are some:

Conserve water. Take shorter showers. If you have a lawn, let it dry out and turn brown in the summer instead of watering it. (It will grow back in the fall when the rains return.) Use native plants for landscaping in your yard and neighborhood; they need less water than a big lawn. Less wasted water can mean more water for salmon and other fish living in streams, rivers and lakes. Conserving water is a good idea, no matter where you live.

Save electricity. Much of our electricity is generated at dams. When there is a demand for electricity, often a new dam is built, or more water is diverted through electric turbines, which can kill young salmon on their way to the sea. When we conserve electricity, we may be saving wild rivers and the fish that live in them.

Don't pollute. We all live in a watershed. Everything you put on the ground may end up in the water eventually. Contact your local environmental protection agency to find out how to properly dispose of hazardous household chemicals like paint thinner, solvents and motor oil—don't put them onto the ground or into drains. Control litter by disposing of it properly so it doesn't end up in a stream. Minimize pesticides and fertilizers; weed by hand instead, to keep those pollutants out of streams, rivers and the ocean.

Don't eat farmed salmon. Farmed salmon are raised in pens or tanks, usually on the coast, where they stay until they are fully grown, when they are killed and sold as food. When farmed salmon escape from their pens, or are accidentally released, they compete with wild salmon for food and spawning habitat, and they can spread disease to wild salmon. Their feeding and medicating can pollute the water where their net pens float. Hatchery salmon, which are not farmed salmon, are raised in a fish hatchery from the egg stage to the smolt stage. Then they are released to migrate to the ocean, and return to spawn in the place where they were released.

Fish with care. If you fish for salmon, make sure you follow the laws and fish legally. Some seasons or areas are closed to fishing. There are many groups that support catch-and-release programs. They teach fly fishers how to select tackle that is less harmful to fish, and how to return fish to the water so that they can return to their spawning grounds. Here are organizations with local chapters working to restore salmon habitat and salmon runs.

Atlantic Salmon Federation Catch and
Release Program
P.O. Box 5200
St. Andrews, NB E5B 3S8 Canada
www.asf.ca

Atlantic Salmon Federation
P.O. Box 807
Calais, ME 04619-0807 U.S.A.

Federation of Fly Fishers
P.O. Box 1595
Bozeman, MT 59771
www.fedflyfishers.org

Trout Unlimited
1500 Wilson Boulevard, Suite 310
Arlington, VA 22209-2404 U.S.A.
www.tu.org

Join an organization that preserves salmon habitat. The following are just a few of the groups working to protect salmon.

The Nature Conservancy buys wild lands to save them from development.

The Nature Conservancy
4245 North Fairfax Drive, Suite 100
Arlington, VA 22203-1606
www.tnc.org

The Northwest Ecosystem Alliance, the Sierra Club and the California Wilderness Coalition all work to save wilderness from development and habitat destruction.

Northwest Ecosystem Alliance
1421 Cornwall Avenue, #201
Bellingham, WA 98225-4547
www.ecosystem.org

Sierra Club
85 Second Street, Second Floor
San Francisco, CA 94105-3441
www.sierraclub.org

Sierra Club of Canada
412-1 Nicholas Street
Ottawa, Ontario K1N 7B7
www.sierraclub.ca

California Wilderness Coalition
2655 Portage Bay East, Suite 5
Davis, Ca 95616
www.calwild.org

The David Suzuki Foundation educates the public and Canadian government on ways to solve environmental problems, and has a Pacific Salmon Forests project.

David Suzuki Foundation
2211 West 4th Ave., Suite 219
Vancouver, BC V6K 4S2
(604) 732-4228
www.davidsuzuki.org

The Audubon Society has a Living Oceans program.

National Audubon Society
700 Broadway
New York, NY 10003
www.audubon.org

National Audubon Society Living Oceans
Program
550 South Bay Avenue
Islip, NY 11751

Trout Unlimited has a habitat restoration program called Embrace A Stream. See "Fish with Care," above, to contact them.

The Adopt-A-Stream Foundation teaches people to work with groups of volunteers to restore salmon habitat. Their Streamkeeper's Field Guide tells how to form a group to clean up a stream, monitor the water quality, and plant native trees and plants for shade beside it. The Field Guide also has the names and addresses of groups doing stream restoration in the Pacific Northwest.

The Adopt-A-Stream Foundation
Northwest Stream Center
600-128th Street SE
Everett, WA 98208-6353
www.streamkeeper.org

Save Our Wild Salmon has many conservation and educational programs to help save wild salmon from extinction.

Save Our Wild Salmon
975 John Street, Suite 204
Seattle, WA 98109
www.oz.net/~sockeye

Carol Reed-Jones is a children's author and music teacher living, writing and teaching in Bellingham, Washington. She and her husband have one grown son. When she isn't writing or on a school author visit, she can be found hiking, backpacking, making wool felt, or reading.

Michael S. Maydak knows his subject well, because he regularly gets waist or chest deep in lakes or streams, pursuing one of his passions—fly fishing. When he isn't out in nature, he is likely to be painting it in the studio of his home in Cool, California. Maydak has been a professional artist since 1976.

Also by Carol Reed-Jones

The Tree in the Ancient Forest. The plants and animals around a majestic old fir are remarkably and wonderfully connected in this stunningly illustrated book. Carol's cumulative verse is the perfect literary technique to portray the wonderful relationship of these creatures.

Also illustrated by Michael S. Maydak

Animal Acrostics, by David M. Hummon. Acrostic poems are a wonderful way to encourage children to write creatively. These "vertical poems" are amusing, clever, and informative.

A Drop Around the World, by Barbara McKinney. Follow a drop a water in its natural voyage around the world, in clouds, as ice and snow, underground, in the sea, piped from a reservoir, in plants and even in an animal.

Lifetimes, by David Rice. From the Dayfly (that lives just one day) to the ancient Redwood tree, this book introduces a great variety of lifetimes and the inherent qualities of each. This book is thought-provoking and fun.

Related Nature Awareness Books from Dawn Publications

This is the Sea that Feeds Us, by Robert F. Baldwin. In simple cumulative verse, beginning with tiny plankton, "floating free," this book explores the oceans' fabulous food chain that reaches all the way to whales and humans in an intricate web.

Salamander Rain, A Lake and Pond Journal by Kristin Joy Pratt. This young author-illustrator's fourth book is a "planet scout's" pond and lake journal—a subject known to be wet and muddy, but fun! Kristin is the teenage "Eco-Star" made famous by her books *A Walk in the Rainforest, A Swim through the Sea,* and *A Fly in the Sky.*

Dawn Publications is dedicated to inspiring in children a deeper understanding and appreciation for all life on Earth. To order, or for a copy of our catalog, please call 800-545-7475. You may also order, view the catalog, see reviews and much more online at www.dawnpub.com.

Dawn Publications
P.O. Box 2010
Nevada City, CA 95959
800-545-7475
Email: nature@dawnpub.com
Website: www.dawnpub.com